When you are at a crossroad this is what happens to you and or your mind. It's September 02, 2015 and I am interrupting the flow of this book already.

I am not sure if I want to up load this book after uploading WHAT ABOUT DECEMBER, but I have to I guess. Yesterday I was tired and like things in my life my dream world changed. For some strange reason I was watching a documentary on Super Volcanoes. This documentary truly annoyed me thus I never got far with the documentary.

Certain things I see on the internet people just irritate my spirit as I've irritated your spirit with some of these books. Hey it's September 02, 2015 and not one copy of these books have been sold (apart from what I buy and give away for free), but I keep writing as if you are a part of my world. Strange but true thus I've told Lovey come October 09, 2015, I am going to indefinitely divorce him. I am moving back home permanently. Listen people I know what he said about my homeland, but in truth, I am living in hell here with him. I would rather go home and face that hell rather than stay here with him in this hell. I cannot comprehend now why I write for him because there is truly no freedom in my life. Yes he does exist but the pain and suffering I feel at times is truly not worth it. I am truly tired and he cannot see this. It's weird, we do for him and base our life and lives off and on him but what good does that do us? What the hell is the point when at the end of the day, you are truly not happy and the avenues you walk in and or try to walk in are closed to you?

All I wanted to do this summer, I could not do. I was blocked from doing it. I am at the stage now, where I need to change and make me happy. I cannot live under the restrictions of Lovey anymore. I want and need to go places and I am hindered. Why?

Yes I know cleanliness people but whose fault is it that we are living in unclean places and or environments? If he Lovey had wanted us to live clean, would he not have built clean? Why give birth and or rise to negative forces if you know you could not control these negative forces?

Do not drill cleanliness into our heads if you as a father and mother are truly not clean?

You can't say you want this for us and keep us dirty? You are going against our WILL and that is truly not right. So as a god, you are truly not fair nor are you right; you are wrong.

People I know the protection of him Lovey and it's me that have to make me happy.

But in all that I want and need to do, I cannot do them and I am frustrated. It seems you have to bow down to and concede to negative forces before anything worthwhile can happen to you. Note that I said worthwhile and not good. Evil isn't good and I fully comprehend and over stand why people do not believe in God.

Why believe in something you cannot see?
Why believe in someone you cannot see?
Why believe in someone that truly cannot speak? No, Lovey can speak so scrap this question. And no, I am not talking about knowledge here thus the frontal lobe of my head is hurting me ever so slightly. Yes the wobbly wobbles come soon, thus my health woes are grave on certain days. Man I've forgotten what

it's like to be healthy and free. These days all I have are health issues that truly won't go away. It's tiring people and I know you too are truly tired of me and my complaints on days like these. *And for you who want to know the wobbly wobbles did come on September 04 and they were severe.*

So out of the darkness I go and leave Lovey behind for my own hell; true hell here on earth. He did warn me but I need to leave the hell hole of this land that I am in.

My spirit yearn freedom my way, but it's trapped in this maze that keeps me locked in. Oh god do I hate life with Lovey right now. Hence I am divorcing him and truly going against him.

Sick of this lonely and depressive world.

Sick of being restricted where I can't do a damned thing. I feel worse than a caged animal thus my spirit is rebelling. It needs to be free of this stressful and depressive world we are living in. I truly hate this life, hence I truly do not want to stay in it any longer. The more I stay in this land now is the more I am going to rebel. It matters not the consequences because **IF FATHER DO NOT LISTEN WHY THE HELL SHOULD I LISTEN TO HIM?** So yes, come October I am so out of here and I truly do not care what Lovey thinks. I have to live for me and

truly forget about him. I given Him my true and unconditional all but what good is that when the one you truly love cannot truly love you?

YOU HAVE TO TRULY GO YOUR WAY. This is why billions do not choose him. Now I am seeing more and I know more than before, so yes, I truly cannot blame people for not staying with him.

You see my struggles and pain and he truly keeps you in it. So why stay in his hell?

You as an individual you have to go out there and make life for yourself. Trust me if you sit around and wait for God and or Lovey to help you, you have a long wait honey. Hence Lovey only helps the ugly and or sinful of this world to me.

Yes I know it's not Lovey that helps the sinful and wicked of this world but Satan. But it might as well be in my book to the way I feel with my yoyo emotions again. Thus depression is a bitch.

No, I am not diagnosed with depression but life with Lovey truly sucks. So before I go home I am going to cut my grey black hair, dye it brown and go start mingling. Dear God no, no clubs. I am so too outdated and I so don't want anyone rubbing up against me.

No, that's not going to happen because I have man repellent that surrounds me.

No, I am not going to go any further because it's September 03 and I am thoroughly confused.

I am lost

So lost that I am drowning in my sorrows

I want to go home

Need the clear waters under my feet

I need, I need (TGT)
Common where are you just about now?

Where are you to soothe my mind with some lovely dub poetry?

Not the shocking or the scary kind but the melodic kind.

No, better yet let me play some **_NASTY by Claudette CP Peters._**

Yes, I need to get on NASTY and wine out mi waise line. Truly love this song. Brap, Brap, Brap because did bam bam gonna shake wicked and wile. And people you need to si di live version of di video. Laade di girl wile.

But in truth people, in all I wrote above I can't leave Lovey and go home. I truly don't know why that when I write certain books like "WHAT ABOUT DECEMBER" I have to come with doubt. Family and people a suh di debel strang inna fi mi life?

Wow.

I know my test of a sexual nature as of late and its bad people. This test we all fail in a way but do we truly? Like I've said, I use Lovey as my beating stick and trust me he felt the punishment rude. So when I am free I am going to dance and get on NASTY in music. Meaning a going to roll di waist an get an wile my way. Music and dancing is a true love and passion of mine. And trust me people; I so cannot dance, so I have to take some dancing lessons if I can.

And yes, I did set in motion my plan to leave and go back home and that plan has been shattered and put on hold as of September 04, 2015.

Family and people, I set up all on the 4th of September, and on the same day my plans was put on hold until 2016. And knowing Lovey, 2016 is going to come an a someplace else a dus go. So for some of us, we can plan an God and or Lovey a wipe out. No matter what we do to overrule him we fail. He is stronger than us.

Yes, I am going to start selling my books now because I cannot incur anymore cost of giving them freely. I am maxed out and tapped out financially. But knowing Lovey this is so not going to happen. I can feel it.

So no more freebies as of this day, September 02, 2015 for which I highly doubt will happen.

Like I said, I was watching a documentary on Super Volcanoes and it irritated me. Thus I went to sleep and I could swear I dreamt my body floating in a sitting position through a volcanic filed. All that surrounded me was volcanic fire and or larva that was like gold. The fire was wow because nothing was in sight, just pure volcanic fire that looked gold that was truly beautiful. I didn't feel any heat or anything; nor did I feel the fire.

Weird but then again I am weird.

Man is my dream world getting weird. I've dreamt so many things and I can't remember if I was in space again and if there was fighting. But I am sure I was to what's happening today. Hopefully I will vent at the end of this book because the bullshit that is happening in this world is getting to me when it comes to refugees. And you know what I am not going to wait until the end of the book because ***NO ONE CAN KEEP***

THE PEACE WITH PEOPLE WHO DO NOT LIVE FOR PEACE BUT LIVE FOR WAR.

The war in Syria is getting to me and I truly do not know why other countries should house refugees (their people) and tax their land, people and economy. *The wars of the East and or Middle East does not concern the West. So why the hell is the West interfering with the devil's own? The law specifically say, "THOU SHALT NOT KILL."* But every day they get up and kill, go against the law and laws of *God; Allah who is the Breath of Life.* Let these people be. They are bleeping death because they kill self and eventually you for death; *A BLEEPING PLACE IN HELL. Thus many developed nations are going to feel it financially real soon.*

Why the hell should any nation HOUSE PEOPLE THAT ARE MORE THAN BLEEPING WARMONGERS? If the Syrian government or any Middle Eastern government wanted peace they would stop the bullshit they are doing. They would stop fighting and killing their own people. *THUS THE DEVIL AND HIS AND HER PEOPLE ARE LIARS AND THIEVES. THEY MURDER AND KILL*

THEN CRY FOR PEACE WHEN NO PEACE IS IN THEM.

IT'S FUNNY HOW THE WORLD CANNOT SEE THE PLOY.

HOW THE HELL CAN YOU SAY YOU ARE MUSLIM AND KEEP FIGHTING; MURDER SELF AND OTHERS INCLUDING LAND AND ECONOMY?

YOU GO AGAINST ALLAHU SUBHANAHU WA TA ALLAH. *So that tells me, you were never the true ISLAMIC RACE BECAUSE YOU DISTORT AND PERVERT THE TRUTH OF LIFE. This is why the BLACK NATIONS OF OLD AND TODAY HAD TO GIVE UP ISLAM. YOU AS THE BABYLONIAN RACE CAME IN AND POLLUTED IT and until this day, we as BLACKS cannot learn to leave you the lying and deceitful jinns and janns of the globe alone. You are the true devils own thus you caused the white race in hue to be cursed literally over and over again.*

You murder at will; so Lovey had to separate his people from you the devils. Satan's own that came in and ruined earth with your war and perversion bullshit of having more than one wife and war including killings.

YOU DEFILE ALL LIFE; THUS PEACE WILL NEVER EVER RESIDE WITH OR IN ANY OF YOU.

YOU KNOW NOT PEACE. THUS THE WESTERN WORLD IS GOING TO FEEL THE PAIN OF DISOBEDIENCE SHORTY, AND CANADA YOU ARE NO EXCEPTION.

No one that is without peace can keep the peace.

If a nation of devils cannot keep the peace in their land, how the hell can you expect them to keep it in yours?

Thus; to the lady that blamed the Canadian government and all governments of the world for your relative dying, bleep you. The Canadian government did not start a war in your relatives land. Blame the government and people of that land. Why the hell should the Western World intervene in wars that were created by them the Middle Eastern and Islamic Countries TO KEEP HELL AND THE DELVIL HERE ON EARTH?

If you as a nation want peace you would not instigate war.

You would not fight amongst your own nor would you kill them.

MORE IMPORTANTLY, YOU WOULD NOT GO AGAINST LIFE; GOOD AND TRUE LIFE.

You say you have the Breath of Life but yet you kill the breath of life globally with your war bullshit. THUS WAR AND HATRED IS ENGRAINED IN ALL OF YOU. THUS EVERY WHERE THE LOTS OF YOU GO; YOU POLLUTE THE LAND AND PEOPLE OF THAT LAND.

Earth does not need you thus IT IS TRULY AND UNCONDITIONALLY FORBIDDEN FOR A TRUE JEW TO MIX AND MINGLE WITH THE LOTS OF YOU.

*YOU DEFILE LIFE BUT YET CLAIM YOU HAVE LIFE. THUS I WILL SAY IT AGAIN, HELL IS FULL OF BLACK PEOPLE AND RECRUITING MORE. AS BLACK PEOPLE **(not based on hue)** WE ARE FOLLOW BATTIES THAT REFUSE THE LEAVE OUT A DI BATTY HOLE OF THE DEVIL; SATAN AND THEIR SEEDS. No wonder many black nations are crippled literally.*

We talk about peace, but yet no true peace is in us.

We talk about life, but yet kill all life; the breath of life.

We talk about God, but yet kill God.

SO HOW CAN GOD BE WITH US IF WE CONSTANTLY KILL HIM AND TAKE LIFE FROM HIM EACH AND EVERY DAY?

THUS WE ALL FORGOT THAT THE DEVIL HAD HIS RACE OF PEOPLE. THUS GENESIS TOLD US OF THE ENMITY BETWEEN THE RACES. And know that Lovey did not put enmity between the Devil's seed and His seed. There was always enmity and strife; jealousy and hatred there. Thus the devil and his people cannot live in peace with anyone. Everywhere they go they create war. They try to blend in and say they are one of us when they are truly not. THUS THE YOUNG BLACK MALE REMINDED ME IN MY VISION THAT THEY ARE NOT ONE OF US. I ALSO SAW THE MARKINGS ON HER.

ALTHOUGH THEY SAY THEY CAN CHANGE, THEY WILL NEVER EVER CHANGE BECAUSE THEIR LANGUAGE AND CULTURED IS ENGRAINED THEM INDEFINITELY.

Hence, no one can change and or reform the devil period and literally.

Sin will always be sin. Thus sin's job is to take the lots of you to hell with him and his people to burn for more than indefinite lifetimes and or until the sins you've committed in the living is paid off you die never to ever return.

My hope now is that Lovey takes his good and true own out of Western lands before this happens. Thus I commission him yet again to never ever give any Babylonian access to our world, land and lands including kingdoms and or abode. Absolutely no access for more than infinite and indefinite lifetimes and generations to come without end. They must go down to hell with their father and mother to be extinguished in hell never ever to rise again. Thus the book WHAT ABOUT DECEMBER Lovey you must adhere to with just and true; honest cause.

There are no back doors here, hence the no access rule applies to all Babylonians everywhere. I am fed up of the lies and killings now man.

24000 years and they are still doing this bullshit. You never locked them out, they locked themselves out of your kingdom and abode and now they want sympathy for the wars and strife they've created. Bleep them.

If the devil had wanted in, they would have said, sorry. They would have said, Lovey, Allah, God, Allelujah, Jah I am truly sorry for forsaking you and doing all that I did.

Not one did this and the is to feel sorry for them after they tainted life and robbed us of you.

Come on now Lovey, don't let me go off on you.

Death is death; it is not life. It is death.

These people live for death; HENCE THEY ARE THE MASTER LIARS AND DECEIVERS OF THE GLOBE.

THEY INFILTRATE YOUR HOME AND THEN DESTROY YOU BY ROBBING YOU OF YOUR WEALTH, LAND AND CULTURE; RESOURSES, LANGUAGE AND DIGNITY, and more importantly, YOU LOVEY. They rob us of you with their Islamic bullshit because you will never ever reside in Islamic landSs because you are not a Muslim but a TRUE JEW.

And if you do not concede to and or with them, they kill you. Well BLEEP THEM BECAUSE ALLAH; THE BREATH OF LIFE IS TRULY NOT WITH THEM. YOUR TRUTH AND BREATH NEVER RESIDED WITH THEM. CAN NEVER RESIDE WITH THEM THUS BOB MARLEY SAID, "JAH WOULD NEVER GIVE HIS POWER TO A BALD HEAD," AND THEY ARE ALL BLEEPING BALD

HEAD FI REAL. *So truly keep them the hell out of the land and lands you've provided for our good and true people.* **_THEY ARE NOT WANTED BECAUSE THEY ARE NOT ONE OF US. THEY ARE NOT JEWISH; A TRUE JEW._** *And Lovey, this is echoed throughout the earth and galaxy; universes everywhere. No hitch hikers allowed. So truly keep them the hell out more than indefinitely. I did not provide for them, so let them be gone forever ever without end. They are not of you. All they do is kill you and have the gaul to say Allah. Hypocrites and parasites are they.*

So Lovey, truly help me to make a true way for us; our good and true people. **_THUS TO THE TRUE JEWS; IT'S TIME TO GET READY. Thus I give you the song PEOPLE GET ON BOARD._**

The Exodus is now. SO LOVEY TRULY LOCK OUT THE HOPELESS SINNER BECAUSE HE OR SHE, INCLUDING FAMILY CANNOT TAKE FLIGHT WITH US. THUS OUR TRUE AND GOOD PEOPLE ONLY BEGINNING 2016,

JANUARY 1 IF NOT BEFORE DECEMBER 2015.

The Western Worlds have been warned. So when they (Babylonians) start on your ass real soon, I truly hope I am not in any Western land to see your destruction and devastation.

NO ONE CAN SYMPATHIZE FOR AND OR WITH THE DEVIL AND HIS AND HER OWN.

The devil will not stop their warring rampage for you to sympathize with them.

LIKE I'VE SAID, A MAN THAT HAS NO PEACE IN THEM CANNOT AND WILL NOT KEEP THE PEACE. THEY KNOW NOT TRUTH THUS THE LIES OF THE DEVIL'S SEED WILL NEVER STOP. SATAN AND HIS PEOPLE INFILTRATED THE KINGDOM OF GOD DUE TO SO CALLED LOVE AND SYMPATHY. THIS SYMPATHY COST AFRICA AND AFRICANS ALIKE DEARLY AND IT IS STILL COSTING US.

IT ALSO COST YOU THE WHITE RACE DEARLY.

THUS YOU KEEP FIGHTING FOR THESE PEOPLE AND YOU KEEP GETTING CURSED AND LOCKED OUT OF LOVEY'S WORLD AND OR ABODE. So truly good luck to you, BECAUSE YOUR

ECONOMIES ARE RIPE FOR THE PICKING; THUS THE WESTERN ECONOMIES ALONG WITH SOME EUROPEAN ECONOMIES ARE GOING TO TOTALLY COLLAPSE REAL SOON.

Eve and or Hawwah as they call her is a testament for all of humanity to see how the devil used her and procreated with her; thus letting lose his wicked and evil seeds globally.

So truly good luck to all of you literally because WWIII will soon be here and if you think the devil will not be victorious over you, you had better think again. The devil did transfer his power to a human and he must rule the lots of you with an iron fist, because he's the new Nimrod of this day and time.

So truly good luck.

HENCE AFRICA, THE SOUTHERN LANDS OF AFRICA YOU HAD BETTER SMARTEN UP AND FAST. THUS I WILL GIVE YOU THE DREAM I GOT FOR YOU AND OR ME AND LOVEY'S CHILDREN AND PEOPLE FURTHER ON IN THIS BOOK.

Michelle

Wow because things are different now. It's August 02, 2015 and this morning in my waking state I saw Dan Dan. She had this thing wrapped around her head. It's more like a thick towel that you could say was in the design of a duck. Strange, but Dan Dan did ask if I was going to miss her when she left; go back home. I guess me seeing her face in my waking state is her way of saying I am not going to let you forget me. I am going to make sure you remember me.

Also in my waking state this beautiful blue, dark blue and white towel with stripes appeared on my door. I would say ¼ to ½ of this beautiful dark blue and white towel with stripes was hanging over the front part and or portion of my door. My daughter went to touch the towel and I said, "don't touch it," and she did not touch it. The reason I told her not to touch the towel was because I was scared.

Weird I know but then again this is truly me. I am weird all around.

My dreams are weird too because I dreamt about Shaggy the singer. I dreamt he brought me these letters and I opened them. I did not hide the contents from him. One of the letter was from a different country. I believe the spelling of the country's name was Cacoa. Do not quote me on the spelling but I know the land's name starts with a C. And for Shaggy to bring me letters, I know something is going to go awry when it comes to me purchasing land and or Lovey's house in the Cayman Islands I think. In the letter, I read denied and then I began to read over the letter. So the purchase I want to make, I was not granted permission to make that purchase; at least so I thought in the dream.

So family and people, if the Cayman Islands deny me access to purchase Lovey's house that is more than fine and alright by me. And people and family this is when I have money. I have no problems with this because if you've read some of my other books, I've been grappling with Lovey in regards to buying his home on this island. Man I've been complaining to him about this. Complaining that the land is not hilly enough and it's too flat. There are no mountains either.

Fam and people, I saw the most gorgeous place in Kenya. This house is simply amazing. It has water in this house, the view that I need. This house is more than perfect, but I truly need a waterfall. Hey I truly don't mind bringing Lovey's home back to Kenya; Africa.

Amazing, amazing, amazing. So I have to go to Kenya because Kenya is that old. The spear they have in their flag is the spear that kills Death;

Satan. Trust me Kenyans don't know just how old their country is. We talk about the Garden of Eden and Ethiopia, well Kenya goes further back.

Kenya is that old fam and people. Thus Kenya is that blessed people and they don't even know it.

They have the key that kills evil. Not just physical evil, but spiritual evil. So no, I would have no issues nor will I have any problems Lovey in building you your mega mansion in this land. To be honest with you, from seeing that beautiful home, I would be more than honoured to bring your good and true life to Kenya once again. But true and good changes must be made in Kenya and African lands. We can no longer give you up and or disobey you. We must truly listen and stop fighting and killing each other.

The key and keys to life is truth Lovey and we as black people must live good and true.

We can no longer side with the devil against you. Africa is losing her beauty because of sin; the sins of the people. And remember Lovey, Mama Africa is tired, so why can't we give her true rest and true peace from the diseases that infest the land, the famine and drought and the economic instability that plague them. But in truth Mama is also a liad Lovey; shi neva lef har European and or Eurasian domain and own. Shi let goh a di West, but shi kip di East and yes I know why, but she must also tell the truth of her own. We cannot keep the truth out of the loop Lovey because the truth is what sets us free, and it's the truth that will lead us truly and honestly to you literally. So yes I know the truth because the West did not listen; they were schedules to fail and fail bad; reckless and rude. Thus the Ying and Yang still resides in China until this day.

Lovey as black people (excluding Babylonians) based on hue and deeds; we have to put away the ways of evil; the devil. The devil wanted us to fail. We the true black race based on hue and excluding Babylonians were to be conquered and enslaved forever ever. This is why death showed me hell in the form of headstones. I know hell is full of black people and recruiting more. Hence you have to lift the ignorant spell that lingers around black people (excluding Babylonians) based on hue and deeds and based on truth also. We as the true black race need to wake up and know *that when our forefathers let sin into their domain, it gave the devil and or Satan and his children (demons of hell) all the right and rights to brutalize us. Satan and the devil as you call him. He and his children can use any means necessary to take us to hell and kill us, and this is what the devil and or Satan have and has done. IT IS BY ANY MEANS NECESSARY THAT YOU THE BLACK RACE MUST BE KILLED BASED ON HUE (EXCLUDING BABYLONIANS).*

Blacks are significant hence the colour black is the foundation of life and death. Life and death come from this foundation, hence life and death began in Mama Africa and life and death also rests in Mama Africa.

Ethiopia is the birth place of Life and Death but we say it is the Birth Place of Life; hence life and death reside side by side. Life and Death joins in South Sudan hence you know Life and you also know Death; thus your White and Blue Nile. Which some call the Ying and the Yang. Now you've graduated from a child; well the kinder garden stage to grade one. This is why you were told about this great river in your book of sin. I believe but not one hundred percent sure; one of your prophets saw heaven and hell side by side separated by water I believe. Well this is your Blue and White Nile.

When I saw heaven and hell side by side I did not see water separating them. Know that this has nothing to do with people in the living per say. Well, well it does. You can say, oh man how do I put it for you not to be confused. I am so going over things I've written in another book. When your bible talks about heaven and hell it's an in transit world if that makes sense.

It's like when you take a vacation and you have to take a connecting flight and you have to wait in transit for that connecting flight. Think of heaven and hell this way in death. *You know your sentence in the grave because before you die; take your final breath and or Black Death yanks or take your spirit or soul from your flesh, you are shown which side of the river you go on. But like I said, I did not see a river separating good and evil even though both worlds are separated. But know for a fact without a shadow of a doubt there is a river. In my first vision about heaven and hell I did not see a river but in my other vision with hell being full of black people I did see a river. Hence I truly hope I've not confused you.*

Like I said, heaven and hell is like an in transit flight where you wait.

Does all people wait here?

No

Depending on the severity of your sins, you go directly to hell.

So if you commit suicide or anyone you know commits suicide, you automatically go directly to hell. You took your own life and it is forbidden for a human being to take his or her own life. Hence thou shalt not kill.

If you bleach your skin, you automatically go directly to hell. YOU'VE TOLD LOVEY YOU HAVE NO RESPECT FOR THE SKIN YOU WERE BORN IN; THUS YOU ACCEPTED TRUE DEATH IN THE LIVING. Meaning you accepted spiritual death in the living; so you must go directly to hell no questions asked. Thus I've told you, HELL IS FULL OF BLACK PEOPLE AND RECRUITING MORE.

Those it things; transgender condemnation it things that my stomach turns at while writing this portion of this book. Oh God are they defiled and condemned in the worst way. God how my spirit turns; is sickened that I have to write about them, but people I have to. These defiled and cursed things go directly to hell. I am not sure if it's the same hell that murderers, thieves and rapist go, but they go directly to hell. They are more than defiled people. A man or woman is not to surgically change their sex to become the other sex. Genetic changes by nature is okay. If you are born with two sexual organs this is okay. It is also permissible for your parents to choose your sex at birth. ***THESE PARENTS CAN***

ALSO WAIT UNTIL YOU ARE OLDER AND MAKE YOU DECIDE ON YOUR OWN. There is absolutely nothing wrong with you. Live your life. *And no, as a doctor you cannot choose for these babies.* You are condemning yourself because you are taking away that parents right. Not because you know nothing about something gives you the right to lie and take away that child's right. Thus you will be punished severely for your actions in death. Stop this wicked and cruel practice. It is not called for. *KNOW THIS, AND LOVEY I AM HOPING I AM NOT WRONG WITH THIS. WHEN YOU LOOK AT AN HEMORPHIDITE YOU ARE LOOKING AT LOVEY.* Meaning you are seeing Lovey in his female and male form. Lovey is female in the living and male in the spiritual. Thus you have him as one in human form. And Lovey, truly forgive me if I am wrong in the explanation of you in this way. Yes I know you are true spirit; energy and it's not easy to explain you in many ways, but this is how I see you in some ways due to duel nature. This is me to you in one sense and I truly love it. So please do not condemn me because you are truly both, but humanity cannot see nor can they comprehend you like I do.

As a male or female that do not have duel sexuality; you cannot get up and go to the doctor and alter your sex. This is a condemnation unto you the people of the land and the land itself. Death can wipe your land off the face of the planet without you knowing. Hence I tell you the demons of hell live for pain. Pain is their natural sexual high. If you think man is perverse, truly don't wait to get to hell because all the sexually perversion you see here on earth combined is child's play to what the demons of hell are going to do with your spirit. I've told you in some of my other books, when you stub and or hit your toe, it is not the flesh that feels it, it's the spirit. **_The spirit feels pain because it is our true life._** The flesh isn't true life. The flesh is just the conduit for the spirit. Once the flesh shed the spirit, the flesh goes back to the earth to be eaten by worms and or maggots, but the spirit moves on to greater and or lesser life depending on your sins. That which you have on your sin record or slate.

So, the doctors and nurses that perform these transgender it things surgeries. Whether these surgeries are in a private or public hospital, clinic or whatever facility you use; you have no chance in hell to see the abode of God; Good God and Allelujah; Lovey. You and your family; children go directly to hell because you aided in bringing condemnation of one of the worst kind here on earth. This act is so filthy and defiled that I truly don't want to talk about it least I become defiled also. So if death wants; death can take everything from your land and sink it also because you have more than defiled human life and life on a whole. Death cannot and will not be charged if death sank your land for this vile act of condemnation alone. Thus I've told you in another book, lands are going to sink literally. They are too filthy; dirty.

I've told you if I am the saving grace for humanity, I will not save anyone that is wicked or evil. So for those wicked and evil spirits that are in transit hoping for a saving grace, and as told to them by the clergy that someone is going to die to save them. Know that you have not a prayer in the world because I would never ever without a shadow of a doubt save any of you. So onwards to hell the lots of you go.

Move it because I save none of you. No saving grace is allotted to the wicked and evil of this earth. The clergy and or church knows this and if they don't know, now they truly know.

___No one that is good can save a evil person.___
When a good person does this, they are prolonging the acts and evil of death. They are telling Lovey they want death to stay on land. They want wicked and evil people to continue their slaughter of humans and all life form and this cannot happen.

So when a good person saves evil, they are going against the *WILL; TRUE GOOD WILL OF GOD; GOOD GOD AND ALLELUJAH; LOVEY HIMSELF.* Lovey is female in the living and male in the spiritual realm; thus 3XY in the physical realm and 2YX in the spiritual realm. And in the spiritual realm you can have 3Y. Y for males and X for females; thus you know why X and Y is used in mathematics. And this is why I've told you in another book that X is not unknown to us it is known. And yes this explanation is wrong because 3XY and 2YX has nothing to do with the physical realm but HAS ALL TO DO WITH THE SPIRITUAL REALM. I just broke things down for you on a physical level because this is all humans know. And Lovey do forgive me for this but I had to give this information on the level humans know things which is the physical.

Until this day they cannot correlate the physical and spiritual. I do not know why humans; we as humans have to put things and or put so much emphasis on the physical when it is the spiritual that is the determining factor of life.

Water and energy sustains and maintains our life. The spirit is dependent on water. All life form is dependent on water and without water nothing can or will live. Without water we are like unto dry bones in a desert. So black people (Babylonians excluded) we gave birth to life and death. Thus Ethiopia gave birth to death; meaning because Ethiopia accepted death long before Adam and Eve, the Blue and White Nile was formed as a reminder of the death we as black people accepted and joined. And yes this is partially why I saw white and blue forming and or being given birth out of the darkness; blackness of life. Originally we did not join death. When Sudan was colonized by Babylon long ago and with the acceptance of Christianity and Islam (religion) they joined death. So blue and white on one level represent death. So on one level, Ethiopia gave birth to death and Sudan joined death; became a part of the six pointed star regime and culture (Babylon). This is no different from so called modern day Israel. None of these lands are of Lovey's good and true kingdom; hence I have to take my hold off Sudan. I truly have to let these people be because it was in this land; South Sudan that good and evil officially joined. *As black people we keep handing over our rights to death.*

We also forget that when we accept death, we accept the nastiness of sin.

WE HAVE TO GIVE UP OUR NAME AND HERITAGE TO SIN AND DEATH. WHEN WE DO THIS, WE NO LONGER HAVE AN IDENTITY. NOR CAN WE IDENTIFY

<u>WITH LOVEY; GOOD GOD AND ALLELUJAH. WE DO NOT HAVE OUR OWN CULTURE AND LANGUAGE. THUS WE HAVE GIVEN ALL THESE THINGS UP INCLUDING LOVEY. SO BECAUSE WE DO THIS, THE HISTORY BOOKS OF MAN KNOWS NOT US. THEY CALL US SLAVES INSTEAD OF THE BUILDERS AND CREATORS THAT WE ARE. WE'VE LOST OUR IDENTITY, THUS WE HAVE NONE TODAY.</u>

WE ARE NOT RECOGNIZED FOR OUR CONTRIBUTION TO LIFE AND THIS IS WHAT'S HAPPENED TO THE TRUE BLACK RACE.

SOME OF YOU TRULY DO NOT HAVE YOUR ANCESTORS LAST NAME. YOU HAVE BABYLONIAN NAMES, HENCE YOU RELISH AND BASK IN ALL THAT IS BABYLONIAN AND OR OF BABYLON.

YOU BABEL LIKE THEM, AND YOU FALL JUST LIKE THEM JUST LIKE THE TOWER OF BABEL OF TIME PAST, NO OF LONG AGO BECAUSE TIME CANNOT

PASS. *TIME IS CONSTANT AND TIME TRULY DOES NOT CHANGE DESPITE THE SAYINGS OF MAN; HUMANS.*

As blacks we had a place and we did have the language of Lovey; God. We gave it up, thus losing our true place with him. Instead of choosing him we give him up and say no.

Now the 18 thousand years of 3X (the three daughters of Eve) is up. And still as black people we continue to refuse Lovey. There are no more chances for humanity at the end of 2015. Man and or humanity must pay according to their works now. All that will be saved is Lovey's own. So truly good luck to the rest of you because come December 2015 the door will be indefinitely closed to the rest of you.

But you mentioned Israel you are saying.

I did.

Because Israel joined the downward and upward triangle Israel became like South Sudan. They joined death and this is why they write and change Death's Book. Your so called Holy Bible. They are not a part of Lovey's good and true kingdom of peace because they joined forces with death and they write books of lies for death to deceive humanity and take them to hell.

And yes this is why in the same book they write Revelations say, "woe be unto the Jews that call themselves Jews because they are of the synagogue of Satan."

So as Ethiopia joined forces with death, modern day Israel as you call them did the same. They lie to humanity saying they are Jews when they are truly not the true Jews. They are death's children; own.

If they were the true Jews they would know that a Jew whether male or female is not governed by the laws of men, they are governed by the laws of Lovey; Good God and Allelujah.

No Jew; true Jew can tell lies on Lovey. A true Jew knows not lies when it comes to Lovey. They know the full truth of him because the truth of Him Lovey is engrained in us. Meaning we have to flee from all that is unclean and evil. We cannot under any circumstances abide with death and the nastiness of their people.

We seek cleanliness, truth, honesty and peace including good health, wealth and prosperity.

And no, wealth and prosperity is not all monetary. Life isn't monetary, thus we live by the laws of God; Lovey and not the laws of man; humanity; well death.

So no Israeli globally can say they are Jews because in truth they are not. They are not of the original descendants of Jews; they are of Babylon thus ABRAHAM A KNOW BABYLONIAN IS THEIR GOD. They tell you until this day that Abraham is their FATHER; thus they had to join death in all that they do. *They had to join the upright triangle to the downward triangle. The six pointed star and or triangle is Death's star in the spiritual realm. They know this but will not tell you this. Thus they do not have Lovey because they joined death. And yes due to lies and deceit their hell is truly not like your hell. All your sins have been poured out on them (these so called White Jews). Therefore, they will find no place on earth that will accept them or save them because of what they have done.*

It is not to say there are no True White Jews because you do have True White Jews. True White Jews can be found in Russia this I know. Maybe this is why I am so obsessed with this land because of the remnants of Jews that can be found there.

I know some of you are saying this cannot be and every negative argument is flaring in some of you. Go ahead and say you are a flake and this cannot be. My family comes from Israel and they are the original Israelites. We have the scrolls to prove it.

And I say unto you, you are a liar and thief.

Israel and or modern day Israel was never the original land of Jews. Ethiopia is.

Ethiopia was and still is the original land of Israel and all of Israel knows this. Let's put it this way.

NO MATTER HOW YOU CHANGE THE HISTORY BOOKS; YOU CANNOT CHANGE THE ORIGINAL PAST OF MAN.

NO MATTER HOW YOU TRY TO CHANGE THE DNA OF FLESH, YOU CANNOT AND CAN NEVER CHANGE THE DNA AND OR GENES OF THE SPIRIT.

NO ONE ON THE FACE OF THIS PLANET WHETHER LIVING OR DEAD CAN CHANGE THE DNA AND OR GENES OF THE SPIRIT. NOT EVEN LOVEY AND DEATH. Lovey cannot go against the values and or morals of life and death. And death cannot go against the morals and values of death. It is impossible thus there is good and evil; life and death.

Death has no morals you are saying.

Death has morals because *DEATH CANNOT TAKE WHAT DOES NOT BELONG TO HIM OR HER. Death can only take what's theirs.*

Thus messengers cannot interfere with death all the time.

Yes we interfere. I've interfered and death, female death gets angry at me. Remember in Haven Hill death; female death specifically reminded me of the 6000 years she still have on earth.

Trust me when you interfere with death you are reminded of it. If you as a messenger continue to interfere with death, death can take you for interference. She can sink your land also. Hence what belongs to death must stay with death. This is the law.

Well I don't belong to death you are saying. And I tell you. From you sin; have more sins on your sin record than good; you belong to death. Your name is written in the book of death.

Stop crying and truly listen. Know your sins. If you don't, tally them up from you are a child until now; the day you are reading these line and or words. You can make amends for your sins. So make a good and true effort to amend or change them.

Listen, despite what I write, you can make a change for you.

Yes I've condemned land and people, but it does not mean Lovey permits it. He does give you time to amend your ways. I cannot change the plight of Babylonians and will never change this. There is no amendment for a Babylonian because <u>*THEIR GOD IS NOT LOVEY.*</u>

THEIR GOD IS THE COW AND ALL WHO FOLLOW THEM AND YES MARRY THEM IS HELL BOUND. THERE IS NO SAVING THEM.

The god of life is not the god of death. Hence the kings of Babylon are the kings and queens for them; of Babylon. Jews must never ever marry

Babylonians but Jews have and has done this. Ethiopia did this and this is why your book of sin said, Israel is no more. I've also told you, Lovey knows them not because it was them that opened the flood gates of hell.

Eve did procreate with death a Babylonian hence she brought forth Cain Abel and Seth. None were good thus Cain killed Abel his brother and lied about it. But in fact Eve did not bring forth boys; she brought forth girls. Evil had to spread and the only way to do this was procreating with a human. Thus Eve (Evening) procreated with Sin; Satan. She let Him in her Garden; her Garden of Eden. So because of this Lovey banished her from his realm; home because she became unclean.

Yes Lovey has girls.

The brides of heaven are all black females.

The Jews are all black females except for 1 bi-racial female.

The chosen of Lovey in the original origin and or original life is black. This has nothing to do with race or racism and or colour of skin. I've told you the foundation of life and death is black thus black must come first.

True life is green because it's the greenness of life that maintain and sustain us; yes the trees.

Blue is life as well because blue is reflected in all that we do. Blue is more powerful, but without blue you cannot have white. White and Blue are side by side hence you cannot get rid of white, nor can you get rid of blue.

Both white and blue are born at the same time. They are twins hence it's unfortunate that you as humans cannot see the birth of life like I did. Like I said, if you were to see the birth of life you would not choose death because it is truly magnificent and beautiful.

Wow because the birth of life is more than a sight to behold. When you see this you want all evil to leave from all around. You don't want to deal with evil or see evil. Yes I know death had 24000 years to violate and kill, but death must be stopped. Death cannot continue to violate the space and world of the good anymore. Also, if Death wanted life, Death would have rejected Sin and amend their dirty ways. Death would have accepted good and true life if Death wanted good for self.

Death and the people of death must go.

Yes I know I've gone in a different direction of this book but this is me. I go off because information given is truly not stable. So much is coming that you can only write so much. And in all truth, much of what I've said is written in other books in the Michelle Jean series of books.

If you want more information and further clarity please get BLIND OBSESSION REBUTTAL – THE TRUTH IS NOW OR NEVER AND A LITTLE TALK WITH GOD by Michelle J. Lyons. These two books are the only one in this series that follow the same format and pattern as the Michelle Jean series of books. All other books in the MJL line are romance novels and short stories.

BLIND OBSESSION REBUTTAL – THE TRUTH IS NOW OR NEVER AND A LITTLE TALK WITH GOD came about because of what I wrote in my novel Blind Obsession and what this Babylonian said to me; hence me being me, schooled him good and proper my way in this book.

Trust me he was schooled because all too often these people think that Black People don't know their true life story. I know the truth of my ancestors. Not the fake and watered down crap they give to us but the true truth. Hence you have these books. You cannot rape me of my truth and knowledge. You can rape and deceive all other black people but you cannot do it to me. I know who I am hence I do not get caught up in the white skin, dark skin, brown skin or yellow skin bullshit. The colour of my skin does not define me as a person. The goodness and truth within me does. Thus Lovey resides in me. Come on now.

Like I've told Lovey, the full and true truth needs to be known and man must know their end. I refuse to butter up or water down anything for anyone.

You have the full truth now as given by me and as found out by me on my own. So live because Lovey did give us true life.

NOT BECAUSE RACE X CANNOT GET INTO LOVEY'S KINGDOM GIVES THEM A RIGHT TO DECEIVE YOU SO THAT YOU LOCK YOURSELF OUT OF HIS WORLD AND KINGDOM.

This is not fair to you nor is it right.

WHEN YOU SIN RECKLESS AND RUDE YOU ARE LOCKED OUT OF LOVEY'S KINGDOM PERMANENTLY COME ON NOW.

*Listen I don't know if this song is appropriate for this book. But I heard this song by **Beres Hammond yesterday called 360 TURN.** Truly* *listen to this song keenly because it sums up everything I want to say.*

Lovey is not a fool so as humans we have to come to Lovey with a better behaviour. ***LOVEY WILL NOT DEAL WITH OUR SINS AND BAD BEHAVIOUR ON OUR TERMS.***

We say we love Lovey, but we listen to hearsay and all sort of crap the clergy tell us to take your soul from you and him Lovey.

The clergy sell you; sell your soul to the devil hence they sould (sold) you for dirty pieces of silver.

Before I forget this dream let me tell it to you right now because this one is weird.

Dreamt black people; males living in slums.

Family and people when I say slum I mean slums. I don't think the worst slums in the world compares to this slum. Wow. Hence I truly don't know people because something is so not right in the black community.

Yes I know the back lash I am going to get for Haven Hill, but you know what, the truth must be told. You cannot have people slaughtering animals in another continent; animals that have done them nothing. ***Hence truly listen to 360 TURN by Beres Hammond. I will not deal with it your way. I will deal with it my way. Hence I took my anger and frustration to Lovey. Hopefully he will deal with it.*** Like I said, humans are savages that cares not who or what they kill to plunge their land and people further into hell. Hell is hot, so why sentence your land and people there?

Don't go there with the killing is necessary because no killing is necessary.

And no one can keep the peace in another man's land. There will always be casualties.

War is war and killing goes against life; hence billions are slated to die. We as humans took it there and forgot that, ***"THE WAGES OF SIN IS DEATH."***

Like I've said in some of my other books, I truly do not want to be a politician because hell is truly waiting for the lots of you.

Well I send my troops into country Y to keep the peace. And I say unto you bullshit. No one can keep the peace in another man's land if he or she sends their troops in that land with guns,

bullets; war machines. You are not fooling anyone. Your intent is to kill and all of you do kill; take lives.

You want to keep the peace keep your troops out of war zones and wars and or fighting that do not concern you. Hence you as a politician go against life because your intent was to kill and your troops do kill. Therefore, there are no peace keepers in this world; only warmongers that intentionally and willingly kills.

And don't you dare go there with religion because no one that is religious can keep peace with anyone. Not because you are a clergy member makes you clean. You're just telling me you are dirty and you are a warmonger also.

Not one of you can tell me anything because death; the politicians of death must go to church to receive consent from you the clergy to kill. Thus politicians consult death all the time before they go on the battlefield to slaughter; kill.

Thus truly good luck to the clergy because not one will or can find a place with Lovey. Therefore I worry not about the clergy because they're all hell bound and condemned just like their parishioners.

Hence Death sells death globally.

Death is a commodity because death is traded each and every day on the stock market of death.

So by me seeing blue and white stripes on a towel someone is trying to tell me that WHITE AND BLUE CAN NEVER BE SEPARATED.

White and Blue go hand in hand thus they are the same. Yes this is odd for me. I know blue is an extremely powerful colour, so what does it have to go with white?

Therefore I have to say I am missing something when it comes to these two colours.

I know they are a part of life and death and they are born at the same time, but what am I not getting with both colours.

I truly don't know.

I know life and death is side by side due to Will. Hence we are given choices in life. We can either choose good or evil and billions have and has chosen evil over good.

I truly don't know sometimes fam and people.

I've been watching a couple documentaries on the internet and I cannot finish them. These documentaries have to do with gangs. Man are they ever violent and I have to ask myself, do these people not care about their soul and the soul of their children; family if they have any?

Hell is real and some of these people say they don't care who they kill.

Some kill blacks because they hate blacks.

Man is the black race ever hated globally. Hence I keep asking, *when is the black race going to truly wake up Lovey?*

When are we going to realize the system of man including men hate our guts so much that our elimination and extinction is inevitable.

Everyone including our own want to wipe us off the face of this planet. So when are we truly going to wake up and have positive growth and wellness in our own black lands?

Wait, what the hell am I saying?

The foundation of life and death is black, so we are not the ones that should leave this earth. ALL OTHER RACE SHOULD VACATE THIS **PLANET BECAUSE LOVEY DID NOT CREATE**

THEM FIRST; HE CREATED THE BLACK RACE FIRST. SO IN TRUTH, THIS EARTH, ALL OF IT BELONGS TO THE BLACK RACE.

WE OWN THIS PLANET BECAUSE LOVEY PUT US HERE FIRST. HENCE HE GAVE US THIS EARTH FOR OUR OWN AND ALL THE REST OF THE POPULATION ARE FREE LOADERS.

YOU FREELOAD OFF THE BLACK RACE.

YOU STEAL FROM US WHAT TRULY BELONGS TO US. YOU ARE THE ONES THAT SHOULD TRULY GO BACK TO WHERE YOU CAME FROM IF YOU CAN FIND WHERE YOU CAME FROM.

And people I am so going to get racist now. Many of you will not like it. Hence I ask you, is racism warranted?

Who the hell are any of you to come into our domain and treat us like shit?

Who the hell are any of you to tell us to go home when earth, this planet rightly belong to the Black Race; us?

Bleep all of you and get the hell off this planet and leave us the hell alone. None of you freeloaders are wanted.

Lovey did not create you first, he created the black race first. This is our home not yours. So get the hell out of our planet and find your damned condemned own. THE BLACK RACE HAVE AND HAS PUT UP WITH YOUR BULLSHIT FOR FAR TOO LONG.

Coo pan unnu tu.
Coo pan unnu.

Unnu hate wi fi wha belong to us.
Unnu caane stan wi because Lovey preferred us over the lots of you. So unnu tief wi heritage, fiwi birthright anna sey a fi unnu.

Lovey gi unnu anyting?

Not one scrap and or square a lan Lovey gi unnu. But yet unnu, come inna fiwi space an tek wey no belong to unnu.

WE GAVE UNNU DAMN FREELOADERS A HOME TO LIVE IN; AN LOOK PAN DI TANKS WEY WI GET. Bunch a ungrateful demons wey nuh ha nuh wey fi goh.

Bitches, we gave your ungrateful asses a place to stay and you have the nerve to slaughter us and kill us. Coo pan unnu to.

Bunch of uncivilized demons of the worst kind that bring about death and destruction in our land. Hence the devil and his children cannot be civilized. Unnu a murderer because Earth was a peaceful place to live in and because WE HAD COMPASSION FOR YOUR UNCIVILIZED ASSES WE WENT AGAINST LOVEY AND LET YOU IN; GAVE YOU A HOME. BIG MISTAKE ON OUR PART HENCE WHEN LOVEY TELL US TO DO , BLACK PEOPLE WE ARE TO DO IT FOREVER EVER. If he says stay away from this person and or race of people, stay the hell away from them indefinitely.

Lovey did warn us about the devil's seed and we truly did not listen. Hence the black race is beaten and vilified, shackled and chained, rape and abused daily by the children and people of sin. They brought their sin and diseases into our domain and look at us the black race today. DISPLACED AND WITHOUT THE VOICE OF OUR TRUE LOVED ONE; GOOD GOD AND ALLELUJAH, LOVEY.

We lost him (Lovey) because we let monsters in.

Monsters that rape and kill us.
Monsters who class us as apes.
Monsters who tell lies on us and our God; Lovey.
Monsters that raped us of our true language.

Monsters that defiled our land and brought sin and shame to our land; good and true home; name.

Monsters that gave us their stinking religion to defile ourselves by.

Monsters that stole our birthright and claim it as their own.

Monsters that intermarry with their own.
Monsters that gave us pork and beef to eat; meat that they knew would defile us and turn Lovey from us.

Monsters that took our clothing and left us bare and naked for the world to see.

Monsters that is jealous of us because of our gorgeous and beautiful dark and white skin.

Monsters who truly hate us.
Monsters who want black babies and can't have none; any.

Monsters that tell us we are not the preferred race when we are the preferred race because Lovey made us first and put us on this planet first.

We are Lovey's preferred stock and race that have and has lost our way. But now it's time to tell every race and creed to bleep off, we don't want your devil's philosophy, nor do we want your devil's religion. Robert Nesta Marley

Hence Duane Stephenson and Taurus Riley you can keep your damned Ghetto Religion because the church can't save anyone. And yes religion can and will be stopped. So keep your crappy song of bullshit because RELIGION KILLS and you are both killing the youths; black youths of Jamaica.

So keep your religious ghettos. _Thus you're both sellouts and apart of the murderers that kill the people of Jamaica including land, for dirty pieces of silver. Unnu a sell out hence unnu KEEP THE ORDER OF DEATH AND SELL THE PEOPLE OF JAMAICA DEATH AND HELL._

Keep unnu ghetto religion.

But noa sey, all that you do to sell death and give your black people death, hell is truly waiting for the both of you.

An yu Taurus, how come yu a sing bout, no because you are not a conscious youth or man. I do not rate you anymore because like your counterparts of death, YOU WEAR DEATH'S SIGN AND MARK ON YOUR HAND. YOU'RE RECEIVED YOUR MARK OF THE BEAST JUST LIKE MANY ARTISTS IN JAMAICA WEY SELL DEM SOUL TO DI DEVIL. HENCE YOUR TATS; TATTOOS SPEAK FOR YOU WELL. No conscious man or woman can wear the mark of the beast on his or her skin or sleeve come on now.

Don't tell me about the ghetto because Lovey did not create ghettos man did. And truly keep the church as your family because at the end of the day, you are one of the deceived. **_Hence the both of you (you Duane and Taurus) keep the order of death and truly sing for death._**

So you and Duane can keep selling death because guess what, unnu hell bound already.

Unnu just need more icing pan fi unnu cake and that's taking the young an ole inna Jamaica to hell with unnu. Unnu need fi mek unnu sacrifice and what better place to do it other than Jamaica because di people dem too fool fool an strupid.

MUSIC DOES A LOT OF THINGS. IT CAN BE SOOTHING, BUT IT CAN ALSO KILL. Thus all that

Bob Marley worked so damned hard for and all that Marcus Mosiah Garvey worked so damned hard for dem people come and destroy; kill. No wonder Jamaica was deemed unclean by Lovey because day afta day we as black people sell him out and lose our pride; good and true way. Hence mi nuh truss black people an Lovey caane truss unnu nideda. Why become broken? When we are broken, what do we as a people have left? Come on now.

From beginning to en wi a sell im out an caane stap sell im out.

Wi sell out Lovey, so why should Lovey help any of us?

We know the law but fail to uphold the law.

Look at what humans are fighting over. Truly look. NOT ONE PIECE AND OR SQUARE INCH OF LAND BELONG TO ANY OF YOU, but yet you have people (Modern day Judas's) in Palestine fighting modern day so called Israel for land. Unnu sey unnu father and or forefathers left you the land.

Bitches not an inch or square inch of land on the face of this planet belong to a Babylonian. YOU HAVE ABSOLUTELY NO CLAIM OR RIGHT TO ANY LAND HERE ON EARTH.

This earth was not created by your forefathers.
This earth was not created by Satan who is your forefather.

THIS EARTH WAS CREATED BY A BLACK GOD NOT A WHITE ONE. Thus all of you fall under the banner of Babylon. So why fight your brother Israel?

Are they not Babylonians like you?
So why fight them for land that belongs to neither of you?

So duly remember a black man came first; was created first in hue; skin colour and hair. Not you or any other race but the black race. So why do you claim land here on earth when none was given to you?

WHAT LAND DID LOVEY GIVE YOUR ANCESTORS?

WHAT LAND, BECAUSE LOVEY I WOULD TRULY LIKE TO KNOW. AND IN TRUTH LOVEY, NOT BECAUSE YOU SHOWED ME A BLACK MAN AFTER THE BIRTH OF BLUE AND WHITE DOES IT MEAN THE LANDS OF EARTH BELONG TO US. NO, YES IT DOES.

All that is on earth belong to the black race, thus you have been schooled in Black Heritage; Truth.

Not your history that the white race gives us to kill ourselves by, but the truth of us, our life lessons of truth that no one can take from us ever again.

So yes as black if they want they can bring HUE INTO THIS BECAUSE LIKE I SAID, IT WAS A BLACK MAN THAT WAS CREATED FIRST AND NO OTHER RACE BUT US AFTER THE BIRTH OF BLUE AND WHITE. But because I know better, I will not bring hue into this. Like I said, THE FOUNDATION OF LIFE AND DEATH IS BLACK AND MAYBE THIS IS WHY SHE TOLD ME THAT GOD KILLS.

I had to find the truth out because in many ways I am ignorant. I am quick to anger and this is why Lovey ignores me sometimes. My anger is too fierce and he has to let me find the truth on my own without the anger. So yes fam and people you can say ya think when it comes to me admitting to my anger issues. Thus I tell you, I do not have the final say in all of this. Lovey has the final say because he's not quick to anger like me. He knows best.

As for my book Haven Hill, wow. That's all I have to say because I did something that was wrong. I admit my wrong; hence Debbie truly forgive me because you were showing me something and I took things the other way around. I let my anger do the talking; HENCE I TRULY MISSED THE MESSAGE OF YOU WHEN IT CAME TO THIS BOOK. SO ONCE AGAIN TRULY FORGIVE ME BECAUSE I WAS WRONG.

Trusting white people in the spiritual realm for me is truly hard and difficult.

I truly cannot trust you guys and I guess this has a lot to do with the history of white people based on hue and deeds; the killing and destroying that this race do throughout the ages and today. So for me, there is no trust when it comes to you. Your race based on hue and deeds are corrupt and vile.

You work for death and in league with death, but it does not mean that when I am wrong I cannot say I am sorry and I am wrong. I have , but my word still stands and my apology is no means a way for you to extend the time of death.

By you telling me that your daughter turned eighteen (18) you were telling me that the time of death is over.

The time of death is truly 3XY thus 3XY cannot be associated with good, it can only be associated with evil; the time for humans to die globally on a massive scale.

3XY HAS ALWAYS BEEN THE WARNING SIGN OF MAN; HUMANS. BUT DUE TO IGNORANCE WE KEEP MISSING THE MARK.

Instead of cleaning self up and doing that which is right to save ourselves; we do all that is wrong and kill self; our self.

Satan had his 6000 years already because he was contained in his containment unit. It was a black woman who released him because she had a child for him. So the one child I saw long ago and wrote about in another book, and your daughter that I saw are one in the same. She and You were telling me that 2 Deaths have and has passed already and THIS IS THE FINAL DEATH OF MAN. THUS I SAW ONE DAUGHTER NOT THREE. So this confirms to me now that the extinction of man is truly before 2032.

Everything is fitting into place. I'm the ignorant one that keeps missing the mark due to anger. Thus I have to calm my anger from now on.

But yet with all this said, I am still missing the mark when it comes to Blue and White. Both colours go side by side with blue being the dominant colour. Meaning there is more blue than white and we see this globally in the heavens (sky) and with the reflection of the seas globally. Thus Heaven and Hell is side by side as we know it. They are joined but I truly do not know why.

Both are linked but why?

Yes I do not have the answer to this hence confusion on my part when it comes to blue and white.

WHY DID LOVEY GIVE BIRTH TO THEM OUT OF THE DARKNESS; BLACK?

Why does blue and white have to be a part of the foundation of life; black?

Why not green like the trees?
Why blue and white Lovey?

Trees do not wage war.
Trees are beautiful.
Water is beautiful.

Maybe the white represents the energy of life; the way in which energy flows.

Lovey when you see a waterfall you see the whiteness of it; the power and beauty of life. So then blue and white cannot be associated with evil; it can only be associated with pure and true life. Thus I saw the beauty in life with the true birth of life. I saw true life being born Lovey and it is truly magnificent; more than beautiful. Maybe that's why I truly love waterfalls. I need a waterfall on the property we have. So in all that we humans do, ***WE BASE EVERYTHING ON COLOUR OF SKIN WHEN IN TRUTH, IN ALL YOU CREATED LOVEY, IT HAD NOTHING TO DO WITH SKIN; THE HUE OF MAN; HUMANS, BUT HAD ALL TO DO WITH TRUTH; THE PURITY AND TRUTH OF LIFE.***

Hence our ancestors of old never got it and today we still don't get it.

Like I said, we created our own hell because we listen to people tell us crap. Thus with the blue and white on my door represent my spiritual flag in a way. I guess I must journey to Scotland because this land house the spiritual flag of life.

I know Scotland has a dark past Lovey thus I truly have to be careful there.

The pieces are there for me to fit Lovey but I get way too angry when things get to me. And in truth, I truly do not feel to go to Scotland. I am so not yearning this land somehow.

Yes I know Satan transferred his power to a human; hence the final chapter of Jesus and or Zeus and or Heysuis has and have come to an end.

I too missed the mark with this.

Lovey, I truly get it and truly thank you. The story of Jesus was a code and I missed this code. All of humanity missed this code literally.

It said Jesus would die to save humanity. But it is not so. No wonder they said, Jesus was the lamb. He was made a sacrifice.

No, that's not right.

Oh man, I truly don't think you want me to explain this to humanity because I truly cannot explain it right without confusing humanity.

This had to do with the United States. Oh man Europe, you're all bitches. No wonder North and South America is separated from the lots of you. And no wonder the bible was commissioned by a European to be written. Screw you with my descent too if you bring it into play here. You're all a bunch of bitches.

How the hell could you do this to another land?

Wow.

Lovey is this the truth though?

Is this truly the truth?

At the last minute you are letting me put the pieces together?

Europe wanted this power so bad that they would destroy another land to get it?

Wow.

France you are a bitch. No one should have power a part from Europe; Eurasia; thus Europa in once sense of the word. No wonder Greece is falling; in chaos financially literally.

The United States never got damn.

Ignorant are they thus they are truly uneducated; not smart at all.

No wonder Africa stayed with you. And to think I gave Mama Africa prayer when she is the one to give birth to life and death in one sense.

She is the hub and womb of life hence we say Mama, Mama Africa. Dem gi bun. No fi real people. Africa a di bunna oman.

No wonder they bible sey Eve was deceived. Shi bun Adam in that sense of the word but this is truly false. Shi neva bun Adam, a Gad, Lovey, Good God and Allelujah shi bun. Shi gi Gad bun to regile.

Shi bun im because shi side with Death and gave over her life to death. Hence you have religion and the churches; well whore houses of death that divide and conquer; destroy and kill globally.

Wow.

So, as Eve gi Gad bun, har wicked an evil children gi Gad bun tu. Thus humans' falla backa death (Pan) until this day.

As for you America wow.

Lovey trusted you with the Upright Triangle and you lost it literally.

You turned the Southern Cross into Death's Cross. See the red and stars people. THIS IS WHY LIFE CAME TO LIFE BUT LIFE REJECTED LIFE BECAUSE YOU'RE ALL IGNORANT.

Marcus Mosiah Garvey came to you to teach you and tell you that you should amend your ways but you did not listen.

You America set him up and deported him. Everything you did to him thus rejecting him.

Now this is where you came in Barack.

You were ordained to take down the devil; kill him because Kenya house the sword of death.

The spear that is in the Kenyan flag is the spear that kills spiritual death; thus you failed to bring down the debt load of America. This was what Marcus Mosiah Garvey was trying to tell you people when he came to America. But instead of listening, you rejected him and plunged America further into debt with Death. *Over 18 trillion dollars and counting. THIS DEBT AMERICA CANNOT REPAY.*

There is no way in hell that you America and your people can repay this debt.

Remember it said, Jesus died so that all could be saved. And I told you, no one can die to save you, they have to live to save you.

Jesus is known as the sacrificial lamb. Well Barack you are the modern day Jesus in America. Jesus didn't save anyone because he was crucified horribly.

He was slaughter between a murder and a thief; his counterparts.

Not even his trusted disciples knew him. They denied him.

Yes Jamaica denied Marcus Mosiah Garvey and sold him out fi rice an peas. Thus the Rasta's of Jamaica and the globe POINT DOWN NOT UP. They cannot be upright because they do not have the upright triangle and never will have it. They are down; point down, hence they are death's clowns and or the clowns of death.

You America house the upward eye in the Triangle thus life was entrusted to you and or in you and you broke rank. So Barack because you were ordained and did not do anything to bring the upward triangle out of debt; hell, you became Jesus of modern day and time. Go to Revelations and read what colour Jesus the son of man was.

He said he died to save people but like I said, you cannot die to save anyone, you have to live. So because you did not secure America's future, and because you've inherited over 18 trillion dollars in death. See the correlation with 18 people. You Barack a black man of bi-racial lineage, but it matters not the bi-racial descent you still black cause yu look black in hue. You as a black man is going to spend the longest in hell of all the presidents in the United States. Yes they forgot to tell you this.

Thus the debt load of America, you a black man in hue have to carry to hell with you.

So multiply the 18 trillion dollars in debt and counting that you have under your leadership by 48 000.

All the men you sent on the battlefield of Death to take another human beings life; multiply those lives by 48 000. AND KNOW THAT THERE IS NO REMITTANCE OF SIN WHEN IT COMES TO TAKING A LIFE. This I know now.

Now because you took leadership over all Americans and because you are their president, their sins (every sin of each American globally) fall upon you literally. Thus for all the sins that each American do, you are responsible for them; thus you are going to burn in hell for all the sins of your people.

Jesus said, he died for all so that they would be saved and since you were ordained and did not secure the life and future of your people, you have to burn in hell for them. So no matter what I wrote in Haven Hill, you have to take the punishment of your people. Thus all Americans globally walk free and you have to go to hell and burn for them. Thus saith the Lord thy God meaning it is so.

So Black Jesus you got suckered big time. All of America walks free and you don't, hence on this day August 04, 2015 I found this out.

You were the intended sacrificial lamb that failed your people literally.

So truly good luck in hell because Death is going to be around for a long, long time.

This is why I keep saying it's not fair for one man to burn in hell and all of humanity go free.

Blacks were always the sacrificial race for whites based on hue, deeds and the acceptance of death by blacks and other races that share the same hue.

Yes this is why she wanted me to go there, New York but I truly cannot. The land is too dirty.

Now you know Jesus did not make himself a sacrifice, he was the sacrifice from the get go.

You were the sacrifice and you did become the sacrifice of death. Thus Abraham sacrificed a ram (sheep) to his god and Jesus was known as the lamb.

Abraham was just telling his people that they must sacrifice you. Thus human's so called holy book is the

book of death and or the code book of death; the book of codes.

So truly good luck in hell Jesus because another of man's prophecy has and have been fulfilled.

And no people I truly do not want to stay long with this book because I got the message and it's been related back to you. Therefore, if you have Haven Hill, this book, Haven Hill must go beside this book.

My Talk Book Twelve – Summary and or Confusion completes Haven Hill.

I've started What About December Book Two but I truly don't know when I am going to complete this book because as of late I've become lazy and truly don't want to write. *Completed and uploaded on Lulu August 31, 2015.*

It's weird Lovey truly weird because in all of this I am boxed in. Any way I look at it Europe won because I am boxed in.

The North fights against the South and the East fights against the West. So it matters not what I do because the East has and have won against the West and the South, I truly don't know who's won there. Thus power is reverting back to the Eastern Block.

So now I ask you this Lovey, why ask me to write when you knew I was blocked in?

If I build your mega mansion and or buy you your mega mansion in the Cayman Islands the Eastern Block would have won due to the Cayman Islands being affiliated with England.

If I build you or buy you your home in Africa; Kenya, Europe would have won because Mama Africa is truly Central Europe from my perspective. Mama Africa did not let go of her White and or European White and Black own.

Africa kept Europe while relinquishing her Western own.

So it matters not where I look because THE EAST MADE SURE THAT YOUR KEY WOULD COME BACK TO THEM BY ANY MEANS NECESSARY.

So as Satan gave a human in the West power, Good must go back to the East and give them power also.

Like I said, I am boxed in because something is not right somewhere. Hence there are no winners in war just losers. People die and for what?

It's the same with you Lovey. You cannot save all because all did not choose you. All couldn't choose you either because All do not belong to you. Some belong to the devil thus many in humanity are going to go down to hell with the devil.

I truly do not want to go to Montreal. It's August 06, 2015 and I dreamt Shaggy again. This had to do with music; a musical contract. The singer had died for some time and in the dream I knew the singer and or artist. Shaggy and I wanted to revamp and or redo his song. I told Shaggy we would get sued if we did the song but he said he could get around it. So I am thinking because the singer is dead he could sing and or redo his song without being sued. But in the dream before the singer died he made a will; well not a will. He made something and or an agreement that said, ***if he died and anyone redo his song, this man would get the first five thousand in sales.*** I can't remember the man's name because I did not get up and write his name down. It's weird because in the dream I was singing different songs that was done already and or sung already.

It's also weird that in the dream Shaggy wanted us to go to Montreal. Yes he had some other singers with him like that sell out Busta Rhymes.

My sister was involved in this dream also. She had cooked food for her church because they were having a church fair. No, not fair, it was more like a pot luck. There's a name you call it but I can't remember the name. Some of the food was covered up in foil paper and some weren't. One plate wasn't but I helped her to bring the food to her car because she was stressed out and could not manage it all.

Wow with the Shaggy dreams. Yes I know this is a dream inna dream but really Shaggy though. Thus death don't stop interfering in my life. Lovey I know certain things in life, it does not take a rocket scientist to figure them out, but in life you have to give credit where credit is due. I will not bash this man Lovey because out of everyone in Jamaica he stood up and he's doing something for the sick children of Jamaica. I look at this goodness when it comes to him and yes I've asked you to bless him in all that he does. ***I know what you are telling me and showing me and despite it all I will not bash him nor will I withdraw me asking you to bless this man.*** Yes Jamaica is dirty but in all fairness, he's the only one that I've seen that has done something positive for the people and country of this land apart from some of the National Heroes of the land.

I am going to come here and go there on this day. Not even, no I am not going to go there with Bob Marley because all he ever had was REDEMPTION SONGS – SONGS OF FREEDOM THAT YOU GAVE HIM TO GIVE TO HIS PEOPLE. It's his people that did not listen with comprehension and grasp the truth of him and what he was trying to tell them.

You did try with us Lovey and despite what you are saying; I know you cannot go against the laws of life. I over stand and comprehend thus war and fighting is never the answer.

Walking with the dead is never the answer.

<u>Truth is the key to life and despite some of us saying they have the truth; your sins that are on your sin record or slate do go against you in the end. Thus Lovey does not play favorites when it comes to Him and the good and true life he's given us.</u> Thus the good some of us do is truly not looked upon but frowned upon.

We all have to come clean I know this Lovey. But how can you come clean in surroundings that are unclean?

Thus the devil will always be with us Lovey because we as humans made it so.

In all that I do Lovey, I have to be fair and just. You and I both know that the Jamaican Government don't give a damn about the sickly and needy of the island and neither does the doctors. I was told to my face when I asked a doctor in Jamaica why does he not go to the United States and work? **_He told me specifically he wouldn't go to the US and work because in Jamaica they get to cut people all they want._** So human life in Jamaica is not valued, thus the class distinctions in hospital care in Jamaica.

So yes I know what you are telling me, but the life of a child is valued to me. When someone is trying to help by doing the right thing then you truly have to give thanks and bless that person. Yes content of character matters to you I truly know this, and yes you are telling me I am going against truth due to cleanliness; **_choice._**

But Lovey, if you cannot bless this it's okay. Do not go against your good and true will; cleanliness for me. You need to do what is

just; right and clean by you, for me and our good and true people. So truly let it go because I have no true intentions of going to Montreal. You and I both know about Montreal and people will not get it. Some will if they've read certain books in the Michelle Book Blog Series. Thus I know the seal of death that he carries.

Thus let's truly leave Montreal off our list of places to visit and or go to.

Yes I've strayed hence Africa did stay with her European own.

So Lovey, I ask you, why me?

Why make me your choice to write you a book if you knew Europe would do anything to get your book of truth; life back?

Yes this is beyond my scope of wisdom now because I am making it so. There is things closed off to me hence confusion on my part.

Like I said, I do not want to choose wrong hence you make the right, good, clean, positive, honest and truly true choice for me. Take back your book of life; good and true life because I truly do not want to give wrong. Nor do I want to fail.

Everyone wants the truth; your good and true life because there is power and truth in you. But yet to get you and or to you, they deceive and kill and I truly do not want or need to be a part of the empires of death here on this earth and in the universe. I would rather walk away from you and it all than give people who do not deserve you, you. I know I am wrong to say this and you are upset at me and I am sorry. But as humans; me included, do we truly deserve you?

Lovey, I too have sinned against you. I too have done wrongs, so why should you even continue to look at me?

Wrongs are wrongs and you cannot change them nor can you erase them. Yes I know we can learn from our wrongs and teach people not to do them. I get this, but are we truly deserving of you considering the amount of sins we as humans do on a daily basis?

But why Europe though Lovey when you knew the West was destined to fail?

Did the East not give the West evil?

So why do I have to go back there?

Yes I know the West accepted death; evil. Thus the offerings of death that the West accepted. By accepting death, the West opened up a can of whoop ass on themselves thus the collapse of the United States is inevitable.

Yes the mind is all over the place and I keep jumping for here to there but I truly can't help it.

It's August 08, 2015 and I uploaded Book 21 in the Michelle's Book Blog Series yesterday.

It's 6:44 AM and my body is weak and tired but I cannot go back to sleep.

Dreaming about death and it's scaring me.

Wow because I just dreamt this skinny lady. I cannot tell you if she's white and or what clothing she is dressed in. ***All she said to me was "THANK YOU FOR GETTING RID OF THEM ONE BY ONE FOR ME," and she shot off an arrow.*** I know there was white paper that the arrow hit, but I cannot tell you if there was a tree. Fam and people I got scared in my dream.

I know what this dream mean. Like I said, I uploaded Book 21 in the Michelle's Book Blog series and I talked about Shaggy and my request. I know shit is going to hit the roof but you know me, I truly cannot worry myself about this. I have a job to do and like I've told you,

Death keeps no secret for anyone. Death have to give up your secrets. It's a must, thus we were told every tongue shall confess and every knee shall bow.

This is weird for me Lovey and Family, My True Family because the Universe who is bi-racial wants him gone and now she's telling me thanks for getting rid of them one by one.

Is this not odd Lovey?

I can feel death in the living because I now know what that feeling was for when I went on my balcony. Someone did fall to their death; two people actually. A young child and a older male at different times. And yes there are more death's like this to come.

Yes this is weird for me thus my body gets taxed sometimes.

Lovey, is there other people that can feel death like this; the way I feel the death of a person in the living?

My body is so tired and I should truly get back to bed.

It's August 12, 2015 and I need to finish this book because death is coming on a massive scale again.

Fam and people I've been dreaming about children; the death of children. I saw this white man in grey and I keep seeing this grey light in my surroundings. This white man was also wearing grey. I also dreamt my father in grey hence I know his health is truly deteriorating.

But what stuck in my dream world this morning are the children. It's as if they were in jail. So I don't know if there is going to me a mass killing somewhere but I know children are going to die. It's not like before when I could tell. This grey light is throwing me off because I truly do not know what this grey light represent, nor do I know what it means to see people in grey; grey suits.

I am use to black and white but now the colour scheme in the spirit world and or my dream world is changing. No, I cannot bust my brain over this, I just have to watch and see just like you. With me seeing my father in grey maybe the killings are going to happen here in Canada who knows. Yes I know I am speculating because death is masking this death if it is in fact a death. It could be something else but I highly doubt it. When death does not want to lose his or her spoils death will mask death and this is what death is doing to me again. So people guard your children globally including here in Canada. Be vigil at school because death is coming again for your children. I know this death cannot be prevented but in truth it can.

Why is death going to take children?

Children are innocent so death should not take them or touch them. This is unfair on death's part; cruel some of you are saying. But death isn't cruel. I've told you in some of my other books that ***DEATH CAN TAKE YOUR CHILDREN AND WILL TAKE THEM BECAUSE OF YOU; THE SINS THAT YOU DO THAT YOU CANNOT REPAY.*** You signed a pact and or deal with death, so death is coming to collect his or her pay. You cannot stop death from taking your child and or children in this sense. So you are the ones to sign over the life of your child to death. And please do not say this is unfair your child did nothing. It matters not if your child did nothing. Death can do whatever they feel like doing. You sinned and the **"WAGES OF SIN IS DEATH."** *So however death collects his or her pay matters not to them as long as they get paid.*

But, but, but God should not permit this. He God is not fair when he does this.

YOU DO NOT BELONG TO LOVEY SO IT MATTERS NOT TO HIM WHAT DEATH DO TO YOU. *You are not his child nor is your child.*

FROM YOU HAVE MORE SINS ON YOUR RECORD THEN LOVEY CONCERNS HIMSELF NOT WITH YOU. WHAT BELONGS TO DEATH BELONG TO DEATH AND LOVEY CANNOT CHANGE THIS TO PLEASE YOU OR ANYONE BECAUSE YOU DID NOT MAKE LIFE (LOVEY) YOUR GOOD AND TRUE CHOICE; YOU MADE DEATH. So truly don't go running to Lovey and call him unfair when your sins are there as proof that you did wrong.

Well he can save us; should save us.

No, he cannot. Lovey cannot interfere with death. I told you, female death is the deadliest of all deaths. She will take everything in her path and if she has to sink your land with everyone in it, she will do it. I know how deadly she is and I've pissed her off three times already. Thus I do not interfere anymore in the spoils of death. Yes the messengers of Lovey can stop her but they too walk a thin line with her. She can and will take you; kill you if you continue to piss her off.

When you can stop male death, she is unstoppable. Therefore man; humans do not know about the difference between male and female death. When we think death we think male death angels and or spirits. Male death is male death, but female death; wow. She is no joke hence Satanist worship female death and don't know it. Don't go there because the five pointed star represents female death while the six pointed star represents male death; well more specifically the union between good and evil. Thus another form of death in the spiritual realm; so don't complain if death takes your child. You did wrong and there isn't a damned thing Lovey can do about this.

I'VE TOLD YOU ALL IN SOME OF MY OTHER BOOKS; SIN NOT AND DEATH WILL NOT COME.

Also the environment that you live in can kill you; cause you to become unclean. I speak about my homeland; land of my birth a lot.

I cannot go there because Jamaica was deemed unclean by Lovey. So because of this; Death can sink the island any time Death wants to.

When Sin and or Death talk about sin, Sin and or Death talk about the United States of America. So Death can break this land free from Canada and sink the land. Or sin can sink this continent all together without sparing Canada due to the sins of America; the United States of America.

I know she wanted me to go to New York and I went to California instead. But somehow America can be fixed financially but I am not one hundred percent sure. She is trying thus the spirit is telling me all is not lost for this land due to the eye in the upward triangle and the Southern Cross, America's confederate flag.

Yes I want it to be over for them but she is holding on. I also know ordinance is there and this ordinance cannot change. He was ordained to sit on the seat of the Presidency but he failed. He failed to bring the debt load of America down. Also, I know I am dreaming about water; the sea but I cannot remember these dreams. I know they are there but they are being hidden from me for some strange reason.

Oh before I go I have to say this. Tony Matterhorn, you should truly stop. How stupid are you to go on the internet and threaten people. YOU ISSUED A DEATH THREAT TO SOMEONE AND THE POLICE OF JAMAICA ISN'T TAKING THIS THREAT LIKELY. You cannot threaten people's live because if anything happen to Nuffy and the people dem wey yu threaten, the police can arrest you because you did issue a death treat; you did threaten these people's lives and your treat was podcast and or broadcasted on the internet for all of humanity to see. I cuss out people in these books. Yes people will come after me to kill me because I know too much.

People will cuss my ass out because I cuss dem out, thus over stepping my boundaries to them.

I even cuss out the Jamaican Government and the day I step foot in Jamaica; jailhouse noa mi because Lovey showed me this.

If anything happens and I so happen to fall from grace; Jamaicans globally, including White South Africans, Germans, Babylonians, Africans and nuff adda black people a goh rejoice fi joy. Truss mi di set up is there due to these books, but I have a job to do and I refuse to walk and or live on pins and needles because of people and the hatred and death threats I will receive.

Billions will not like me but as long as Lovey truly loves me and protects me I am truly good to go. Evil has a job to do and they do do it; their job. **So Matterhorn, IF YU NOA SEY YU LIVE INNA GLASS HOUSE, WHY ARE YOU THROWING STONES? YU NOA SEY YU CAANE TEK BLOW SOH WHY ARE YOU THROWING BLOWS? <u>Glasshouse Peter Tosh</u>**

You do not threaten to kill a man for his words. Yu call others fish, soh why now it a affek yu?

Yes words do hurt but yu choa dem, so tek dem. Just like me when my time comes. I have to take my blows. Yes I have my visions of what I see, I have the records of humanity to stand on, plus I have the internet to show me things.

It's word fi word Matterhorn, not word fi death. Yu cannot kill a man because dem retaliate and touch yu an eee sting yu.

It's so weird that when some a unnu choa unnu dutty wud dem and people fling bak blow an sting unnu, unnu draw fi di gun anna threaten people life. Yu started the frak business suh wen people done you, you cannot complain. Tek yu loss an blow like a real man. Jus lap yu frak tail an come again.

These people did not threaten your life; you threatened theirs from what I saw on the internet. So in essence they can charge you for uttering death threats. And don't say you did not threaten dem life. Your rant and tirade on the internet gave you away.

Yes as Jamaicans some a wi head hot an wi dark sometimes as well as ignorant. I am because I get off on people and these books are there to prove this. Ole people sey, WORD IS WIND.

PETER TOSH SEY, "IF YU LIVE INNA GLASS HOUSE DON'T THROW STONES AND IF YOU CAN'T TAKE BLOWS BROTHER DON'T THROW BLOWS. Harm no man, let no man harm you. Do unto others as they would do unto you."

Hence give respect where respect is due and people will respect you.
So because of your violence tirade, hang up yu frak. And yes mi laugh when Vegas a chat because he is so correct even though mi truly nuh like im.

Stick to DJing because yu took fish rant way too far. Yu get knock and Matterhorn your house came tumbling down period.

As for you Gully Bop. Wow.

Yu si pump an pride is a sin. Humble yuself. Yu buss again but di fifteen minutes wey yu get soon dry up. As for the management team that backed you, you should have known they were thieves.

Yu shoulda tek a page from Joe Bogdanovich how tief di people dem in Isaiah Laing camp was. Now your image is tarnished and some people think of you as a clown; me included. Yu get out a di gully, wey yu waane guh back inna di gully fa? Listen, the entertainment business is full a crooks wi all know this. You know this as well. Everyone a look food and it matters not how dem get it so long as dem get it. Yes it's a shame that business is like this globally, but we were told people will sell their souls for money and many have and has especially in the business you are in.

Some people bow.

Some people make sacrifices.

Some people kill.

Some people butt tun up and spread out fi money.

Some man and some woman turn prostitute whether they are called gigolos or not, they are still male prostitutes that sell self for money. **_They are a commodity because they can be bought and sold._** *So yes dem a stock market* *except they are not on Wall Street. But then again you never know. They could be traded under the quiet under the drug and or pharmaceutical isle.*

What I am saying is, the world is changing and in order for humans to achieve and reach anywhere, many sell you death and this is truly a shame. In Jamaica dem rab yu blind and if dem can suck out di teeth dem wey inna yu head dem wi dweet. Yu noa wha, Joe Bogdanovich mi dey pan yu case because sey yu a puppet inna Jamaica to regile.

Your company is bust and to be honest di people dem wey yu had around yu nyam yu out, tun yu dung and left you hanging. Thus I still say you need to walk di plank.

Wow because we talk about ghetto but you truly surpassed ghetto. I have to truly say I am ashamed for white people when it comes to you. **_Coo pan wey yu a fight ova._**

Wow became some man truly nuh ha shame to rass. An I only thought it was some black man wey nuh ha shame but yu tek di cake.

Yu ha a beautiful son, look after him because when it's all said and done, yu nuh ha nuh use and you were just a game to be played and had. Your gorgeous and beautiful son deserves a future and he does deserve better, so act like a father and stop acting like some rev out sketel that is scrapping the bottom of the barrel for affection. Cratches anno all because decent oman dey; but den you wouldn't know that from your actions. ***STOP ROBBING YOUR CHILD OF HIS FUTURE.***

Reggae in Jamaica is not relevant because people truly do not buy some of these artists CD's. None tun up thus many artists in Jamaica degrade themselves and people abroad look upon you as a damn idiot. Yu fool fool nuh rass thus you are just hanging unto a thread when it comes to your bank account. Give your son a proper future and lef di dutty pum pum dem alone. It's beyond me why some men degrade demself with women that wuss dan merry go roune to regile. Dis man, dat man, datdey one dey, Tom, Joe, Harry, Barry, Jerry, Frank, Luscious and you name it, guh dey and stab it out and di ole wurl noa bout it, but yet yu defen it. Di mileage high to rass and yu nuh sink inna it. Wow. A Jamaican oman. A suh yu lang lacka and haade lacka. Blurnaught. Wow hence truly provide a future for your son because he deserves it. At the end of the day, he's your true blood and it's not fair for you to bruk dung im future jus because di oman dem wey yu ha a nyam, sarry a buk yu dung. Ghetto sell for some people but not all. Yes uptown go downtown but in your case, the going down on your part is a disgrace. Find reputable artists that will uphold your integrity on an international scale not rev out sketels that sell demself like whores and prostitutes and think the world is going to buy their garbage for long. Stop letting people like me look down on you because at the end of the day, **THE DOWNSOUND SOUND BRAND DO NOT SELL.** *YU A NYAM OUT, THUS YOUR DWINDLING BANK ACCOUNT LITERALLY.*

Grow up and have some sense. Rebrand because soon filth will not sell. Earth is aligning for major destruction globally and if you are not clean you will be devoured; be lost at sea like most of the people dem wey yu associate with.

People and or humanity globally have to start walking away from their sins and memba sey, due to the killing of a lion there is no remission of sins for death; murder; sacrifices; bleaching of skin. Soon there won't be any remission of sin for prostitution; the selling of self on the streets, musically and artistically. Remember death is death and soon di dead a guh talk. It's just a matter of time.

Yes fam and people I had to put that in this book because like I said, destruction cometh on a massive scale and I truly do not want to be some of you people.

Monkeys, monkeys, monkeys, apes, apes, apes; I am so not sure but America you need to be on high alert. Allelujah because something bad is going to happen in your land.

Wow Allelujah.

May Lovey truly have mercy on you because you are truly doomed. So for those who can leave, Lovey truly let the EXODUS BEGIN FOR YOUR GOOD AND TRUE PEOPLE. IT'S TIME PEOPLE, IT'S TIME TO LEAVE OUT OF BABYLON.

Lovey wow

Glory, mi belly, mi belly, mi belly.

Woe mi belly, mi belly, mi belly, mi belly.

America your cup overflows hence the contents of death has been poured out on you.

Have mercy Lord because death must get their pay on a massive scale. She can no longer save a nation that gave you up Lovey. Death has this land locked, hence I will not go there to please her. Every man woman and child that is of you Lovey must now prepare to leave because this land is going to be destroyed literally.

Let the Exodus begin Lovey. You need to save your people thus let Canada, the Southern Lands of Africa with the exception of South Africa for white people, Scotland, Russia; the lands you deem clean and worthy, **_let them give your good and true people and your good and true people only a home._** Lovey we have to secure lands and funds for our good and true people so that when death comes on a massive scale; they are well secure in you and well taken care of financially, health wise and food wise including water wise. We have to be there for our people because the feel I have is truly not right.

**It's September 05, 2015 and this morning I dreamt the map of Africa. On the map certain countries in the Southern Lands of Africa was being outlined in a fiery gold and or gold. Lands like Botswana but not South Africa or Lesotho or Swaziland. It was lands on the left of the map going upwards and out.**

I also dreamt this dirty river that had boats in it. Rows of boats but no people and or no one was in these boats. They were just there in the dirty water. Fam and people, I looked on the internet to see if I could find the boat in my dream but could not. The boats were like unto fishing boats but bigger and without the top on it.

I truly do not know what these dreams mean, but if you know please let me know.

To surmise, I know the bible talks about walking on gold when you get to heaven but this is a lie.

ABSOLUTELY NO ONE KNOWS WHAT THE INSIDE OF LOVEY'S ABODE LOOKS LIKE; NOT EVEN ME.

If you are not truly clean how can you say this is what the inside of Lovey's abode look like?

Do spirits walk with their feet flat and or firmly on the ground like humans?

Does Lovey, Good God and Allelujah walk like a man and talk like a man in his true form?

So how do you know that Lovey's abode is lined with gold?

I know for a fact that Lovey does not deal in gold in that way.

Now tell me and Lovey too, what material possession you take with you to the spirit realm and the abode of God; Him?

Is the abode of Lovey physical or spiritual? And truly do not go there with Lovey's house.

This house could be a gateway to him in the physical. And to say this is wrong because I truly do not believe in superstitions of men and women. I know life, thus its facts I deal in; that which Lovey shows me, and that which I find on my own. **<u>Thus the spirit world leaves me to find things on my own.</u>**

So to say Lovey's abode is lined with gold is a grave sin. The gold I saw in my vision hath to do with Mama Africa. I was shown a map of Africa and the borders of different countries were outlined in gold for which I call fiery gold. It is that beautiful and bright.

Let me get a map of Africa and embed it here.

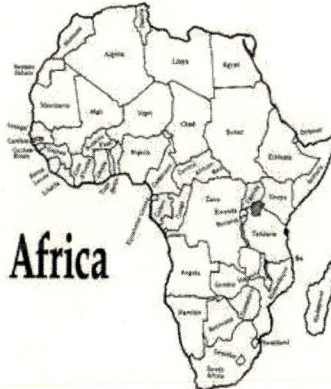

So the gold outline I saw started with Botswana, going towards Namibia to Angola. I cannot

remember if Gambia was included but you get the picture. **_So if heaven is paved in gold, then that gold must be the Southern lands of Africa. THUS MAKING AFRICA; THE SOUTHERN LANDS OF AFRICA HEAVEN._** Therefore, heaven is truly here on earth and no place else. So truly good luck to the rest of the world because your borders were not being outlined in gold.

Like I've said over and over again, the black race have and has been colonized by everyone and it's time that we as a people stop letting our land and lands be colonized.

When this happens (colonization), these different nations infuse their culture, customs, language and values into our own; thus diluting our life; our truth. Hence our rich history, lineage and pride is stolen; degraded, whilst theirs we have to take and be indoctrinated in and this is wrong. Do not come into my land and force me; by beating me to take on your nasty and corrupt values. Thus in the new world that is coming, none of you can come in with your Babylon, Russian (And in truth Russians are not pure blood, you are all mixed with black whether you like it or not. The hair on some of your heads including facial features tell the tale.), French, British and whatever have you bullshit. Thus the pretty skin of some of you.

This new world that is coming is not about your nasty and vile game and games. It's about cleanliness and truth and if you are not clean, honest and true, there is absolutely no way you are going to get into this new world.

As blacks when we let everything go, what do we have left as a people; nation?

We are not one of them because we as blacks are treated like second class citizens. All was taken from us and until this day we cannot see it. We are the ones to dilute ourselves. We say we are all Africans and we are not all Africans. Africa is the womb and center of life; the navel but it's not all black people come from there. The first black man I did not see the land; physical land he came from. All was dark around him and despite me thinking he was not attractive, by no means mean that he was not. In truth, I truly do not find Will Smith attractive nor do I find all American men attractive. Listen people, I truly love a bulky man. I'm a Mark Henry and Bobby Lashley type of girl. These men are cute and attractive to me and for me. I truly love powerhouse men; strong men. Hey the butt people, the butt. Damn I can just squeeze it all day. Oh sorry, I am going crazy. But yes the butt will do. Onwards I go.

All that is Pagan we accept and when the truth finally comes, the majority of you will continue on with you foolishness of accepting deities that has nothing to do with us; nor do they have anything to do with God; Lovey.

Many of you worship men and say these men are your gods. ***THEY ARE BLEEPING DEAD, SO HOW CAN THESE DEAD MEN BE YOUR GODS?***

Are they saving you right now?

Are they answering your prayers?

Now tell me, WHAT DID THESE DEAD MEN THAT YOU SAY ARE YOUR GOD AND GODS CREATE?

IF THEY WERE GOD AND OR A GOD, WOULD THEY NOT BE ALIVE?

WOULD YOU BE SLATED TO DIE?

WOULD YOU NOT BE LIVING WITH YOUR GOD IN TRUE PEACE AND HARMONY?

MORE IMPORTANTLY, WOULD HE NOT SAVE YOU FROM ALL THAT IS WICKED AND EVIL?

Don't go there because Lovey is not dead. He's not human in that sense, thus he left us with all that we need. And like Bob Marley said, **"THERE IS A NATURAL MYSTIC BLOWING IN THE AIR, AND IF YOU LISTEN CAREFULLY NOW YOU WILL HEAR."**

So if you don't know Lovey, you cannot hear him nor will you be able to see him. This man (Bob Marley) told you everything that he knew, but none; not even his own comprehended him. Ignorant are they. Thus Jamaica is doomed. Did not change their dirty and filthy ways of wickedness and sin.

As black people we don't need to belong nor do we have a need to belong. Lovey saw it befitting to make the first human male black. No one can take this from us. No matter how they hide the truth, we will find it because the truth is in us, and none can change their true history and or life story.

NO ONE CAN TAKE AWAY THE BLACKNESS OF LIFE. NONE CAN KILL IT EITHER BECAUSE WHEN ALL LIFE IS GONE, BLACK, THE BLACKNESS OF LIFE WILL STILL BE THERE. SO NO MATTER HOW THEY TRY TO ELIMINATE US THE BLACK RACE, THEY ARE ELIMINATING SELF ALSO BECAUSE IN TRUE TRUTH, THE BLACKNESS OF LIFE WILL NOT

MAINTAIN OR SUSTAIN THEM. THEY KILLED LIFE PERIOD.

ALL LIFE FORM IS DEPENDANT ON THE BLACK RACE; BABYLONIANS EXCLUDED BECAUSE THEY ARE TRULY NOT FOUND ON THE MOUNTAIN OF LOVEY AND THEY ARE TRULY NOT INCLUDED IN LIFE DUE TO THEIR LIES AND DECEIT.

For some the truth lays dormant, but when it's awaken no one can take that truth from you.

THUS TRUTH IS EVERLASTING LIFE.

So it's time to wake up black people because you are sleeping like and with the dead.

Yes what they did to this man was truly wrong. But Lovey, my word stands in WHAT ABOUT DECEMBER – BOOK TWO. No black male, whether woman or child should be made a sacrifice and a pawn for no one; and or anyone. Everyone is responsible for their own sins and another nation should not come in and lie; deceive another race **JUST BECAUSE THEY WERE COMMISSIONED TO HELL. THEY THE SO CALLED WHITE JEWS KNEW THEY WERE HELL BOUND, SO YOU MADE UP JESUS TO FOOL THE WORLD AND SEND HUMANS**

GLOBALLY TO HELL. What right do these people have to do this?

What right do they have to send all of humanity to hell with them come on now?

YOU SAID A BLACK MALE WOULD SAVE THE WORLD BECAUSE YOUR DESCRIPTION OF JESUS IS BLACK. BUT THIS WAS FAR FROM THE TRUTH. YOU MADE A BLACK MAN ACCEPT THE DEATH OF HUMANITY. NO, YOUR SINS.

Now all of humanity believe in the Jesus lie and bow down to Jesus. Worship him as their god and saviour.

THIS BLACK MAN WAS YOUR SACRIFICE TO DEATH IN HOPES THAT DEATH WOULD NOT TAKE YOU AND OR THE BABYLONIAN RACE. SO YOU LIE TO HUMANITY TO SAY YOU ARE JEWS WHEN YOU ARE NOT.

You lied because you thought if you got this man to accept the sins of humanity (America) all would be okay with you, and you would get into

Lovey's kingdom. You would not go to hell because someone accepted your sins for you. Thus the wages of your sins would be paid.

BUT GUESS WHAT.

LOVEY TRULY KNOWS YOU NOT.

HEY YOU WON BECAUSE THE BLACK RACE DID FOLLOW YOUR LYING WORDS TO A TEE ALL THE WAY TO HELL.

THEY ARE GOING TO BURN BECAUSE THEY DID REJECT LOVEY AND ACCEPTED YOU.

UNFORTUNATE BUT TRUE; THUS HELL IS FULL OF BLACK PEOPLE AND RECRUITING MORE LITERALLY.

So as your cup poured OUT on Barak a Kenyan by lineage and descent, so is his cup poured out on you more than 2 to ten folds. All that you have given him (the sins of America and its people) must come back to you.

You knew the spear of Kenya kills evil in the spiritual world. Thus you had to give Kenya death, but in truth Kenya was spared your vileness and vile actions. Lovey will always remember Kenya because a Kenyan was truly good to me and the truth that I have with Lovey, Good God and Allelujah is more than indefinite and forever ever without end.

You knew Kenya is that old, older than Ethiopia in my book. Thus the spear of death was bestowed upon them.

So by doing what you did, you think death would pass from your land and take Kenya but it will not work.

No Kenyan on the face of this globe and no African, no because some lands in Africa truly does not belong to Lovey so I withhold no African; thus no Kenyan or another black man, woman and child (those that fall under the banner of God, Lovey; Good God and Allelujah) will take on your sin and sins. So truly go to hell and burn bitches. Keep your Babylonian stench and empires because I more than take Lovey's hand in more than unity and true and unconditional love of truth and indefinitely lock all of you out of our good and true abode; land and lands including kingdom and kingdoms everywhere including the known and unknown universe and universes; galaxies. No entry is given to the lots of you because your time is up; truly over indefinitely.

Keep your hell because hell is where you belong and hell is where all of you are going to go.

You sinned and you must pay the price for your sins. No one is commissioned to be your scapegoat. Lovey never commissioned anyone to and He never will.

You lied against Lovey and you must pay the price for your lies.

You indoctrinated the globe in your Babylonian lies, thus leaving humanity CONFUSED, RAPED AND WOUNDED; DEAD.

You left humanity for dead. So as you emptied your pain and suffering on a black man; black human male; so is his sorrows and pain and the sorrows of the world emptied back on you more than ten folds.

Grave is your hell and you alone must go there. Thus your hell is different from the people you've sent to hell to burn and die. Thus saith the Lord thy God meaning it is truly and indefinitely so because it is written. Thus this ruling is commissioned against you ad this ruling must take effect by the end of 2015 and move forward indefinitely without end. So as you commissioned man; humans globally to die, you must also die with them because of your lies and deceit.

Everyone has a right to live. You do not take a man's right from them. And not because I say I will not save wicked and evil people and certain lands, it does not mean Lovey will not save them; let them find a way to him.

We all have a choice in life and none must coerce anyone and take their life from them.

There is right and wrong thus humans know better but do not do better for them.

Like I've said, Lovey has tried, we are the ones that don't want to give up death.

Why?

Living good does not mean you cannot have fun. Go to the club if you are a club goer. Have your fun **but do not pick up or try to pick up someone if you have a mate and or your special some at home.** *If you do (try to pick up someone and you have someone already) YOU* **WOULD HAVE SINNED HENCE DIRTYING YOURSELF.**

Know that when you are walking with Lovey and you are doing wrong, Lovey will tell you just as how he's told me. I am stiff necked too. Hence I battle him for Jamaica in my way and you read and know this. Jamaica is engrained in me but the lies and whoredom of the people in the land, I truly cannot take. Yes I am hoping for a positive and good change in my life because I feel stuck in this land. Thus I truly want to rebel against God: Lovey, Good God and Allelujah.

So in all that I write, Lovey is the final sayer and commissioner in all of this.

24000 is the time of death. Within that 24000 everyone including evil had a chance to amend their ways and because of greed and hatred you (Babylon) turned the entire global nation against the truth; Lovey. Thus one (1) cycle of death is every 24000 years for the mass extinction of life no matter how small in number that life is.

Lovey did you nothing thus THE WAGES OF SIN IS DEATH AND THE LOTS OF YOU ARE GOING TO DIE, BECAUSE A DIFFERENT AND MORE PAINFUL DEATH IS WAITING FOR THE LOTS OF YOU.

*So black people, smarten up and stop letting different nations come in and use you. You know the truth as well as know the false offerings of them. **If you have Lovey stay with him BECAUSE ONE DAY THE STORM WILL BE OVER. It's over now, THE STORM IS OVER NOW, so truly prepare yourself and leave out of Babylon until it's safe to return.** The*

Exodus begins now so do all to find your place in your new home.

Maybe this economic collapse is going to be good for America who knows. All I know is, despite me wanting America to crash and burn my spirit tells me otherwise.

I just have to wait and see because at the end of the day, I truly think something and or someone good is going to come out of you and repair the damage that was done to you.

As for my writings, I am not sure if this is my last book.

Yes I am tired and I feel as if I've come to the end of my journey but who knows.

We will truly see.

You know it's amazing how you tell some black people the truth and dem swear up an down sey a lie you a tell. All when di information a slap dem inna dem face dem still a sey a lie.

Aye sah psychological conditioning is a bitch eee noa. Thus the black race have and has been conditioned to think they are inferior to the white race. Thus what they give us as the truth is what we accept without thinking. Bob Marley

*None has truly thought about our historical truths. Now tell me, if there's only a **WHITE GOD, WHERE DID THE BLACK RACE COME FROM?***

How did we come into being? And none of you better bring the ape and or monkey bullshit to me because I've never seen a animal and or ape and or monkey produce a human child.

No whack job and whacked out lunatic of a so called scientist that study animals can come to me with the bullshit of how humans are close to apes in the evolution department. Maybe you are, but none in humanity are close to animals. Take your bullshit someplace else and stick it.

*It's time to stop screwing up humanity with your lame ass bullshit. **You know not creation therefore you know not about life.** THIS IS WHY YOU LIE AND DECEIVE WITH YOUR SCIENTIFIC BULLSHIT. GOD HAS AND HAVE LEFT YOU, SO YOU SPREAD YOUR LIES OF BULLSHIT AND DECEIT; GREED.*

Hence I constantly drill it in your heads that death has nothing to do with life. Death is death and life is life. We as humans are the ones to accept death thus death is in our DNA; genes.

Can you get rid of death?

Sin not and death will not come around you; Death will be gone and eventually gone from your spirit; DNA and or genes. YES GENES IS (genesis).

So as I come to the end of this book, truly live for you and do all that is good and true for you.

In all that you do, forget the hue of man and or self because in truth, the hue of man is not life and it cannot get you into Lovey's abode.

Your history is your history; truth and if you are a mixture of race, embrace both your cultures. In all I write it's truly not based on skin tone and or the colour of skin but based on life; the true you which is your spirit. When you live wrong here on earth, it's not the flesh that pays the penalty or the price in the end; it's the spirit. Thus 48000 years is allotted for one sin and this is because we are both physical and spiritual. Yes some sins are automatic death, but it does not mean there isn't a time frame allotted for and or to automatic deaths.

So truly know you and your sins and try to amend them if you can.

Michelle Jean.

OTHER BOOKS BY MICHELLE JEAN

Blackman Redemption – The Fall of Michelle Jean
Blackman Redemption – After the Fall Apology
Blackman Redemption – World Cry – Christine Lewis
Blackman Redemption
Blackman Redemption – The Rise and Fall of Jamaica
Blackman Redemption – The War of Israel
Blackman Redemption – The Way I Speak to God
Blackman Redemption – A Little Talk With Man
Blackman Redemption – The Den of Thieves
Blackman Redemption – The Death of Jamaica
Blackman Redemption – Happy Mother's Day
Blackman Redemption – The Death of Faith
Blackman Redemption – The War of Religion
Blackman Redemption – The Death of Russia
Blackman Redemption – The Truth
Blackman Redemption – Spiritual War
Blackman Redemption – The Youths
Blackman Redemption – Black Man Where Is Your God?

The New Book of Life
The New Book of Life – A Cry For The Children
The New Book of Life – Judgement
The New Book of Life – Love Bound
The New Book of Life – Me
The New Book of Life – Life

Just One of Those Days
Book Two – Just One of Those Days
Just One of Those Days – Book Three The Way I Feel
Just One of Those Days – Book Four

The Days I Am Weak
Crazy Thoughts – My Book of Sin
Broken
Ode to Mr. Dean Fraser

A Little Little Talk
A Little Little Talk – Book Two

Prayers
My Collective
A Little Talk/A Time For Fun and Play
Simple Poems
Behind The Scars
Songs of Praise And Love

Love Bound
Love Bound – Book Two

Dedication Unto My Kids
More Talk
Saving America From A Woman's Perspective
My Collective the Other Side of Me
My Collective the Dark Side of Me
A Blessed Day
Lose To Win
My Doubtful Days – Book One

My Little Talk With God
My Little Talk With God – Book Two

A Different Mood and World – Thinking

My Nagging Day

My Nagging Day – Book Two
Friday September 13, 2013
My True Love
It Would Be You
My Day

A Little Advice – Talk
1313, 2032, 2132 – The End of Man
Tata

MICHELLE'S BOOK BLOG – BOOKS 1 – 20

My Problem Day
A Better Way
Stay – Adultery and the Weight of Sin – Cleanliness
Message

Let's Talk
Lonely Days – Foundation
A Little Talk With Jamaica – As Long As I Live
Instructions For Death
My Lonely Thoughts
My Lonely Thoughts – Book Two
My Morning Talks – Prayers With God
What A Mess
My Little Book
A Little Word With You
My First Trip of 2015
Black Mother – Mama Africa
Islamic Thought
My California Trip January 2015
My True Devotion by Michelle – Michelle Jean
My Many Questions To God

My Talk
My Talk Book Two
My Talk Book Three – The Rise of Michelle Jean
My Talk Book Four
My Talk Book Five
My Talk Book Six
My Talk Book Seven
My Talk Book Eight – My Depression
My Talk Book Nine – Death
My Talk Book Ten – Wow
My Day – Book Two
My Talk Book Twelve – What About December?
Haven Hill
What About December – Book Two